THUNDER

IN MY

SOUL

a collection of illustrated poems

Norma Slack

Published by Norma Slack

First published in United Kingdom in 2018

Printed by CreateSpace

Visit the author's website at www.normasue.com

First Edition

To Keith.

My constant.

π

"Painting is silent poetry, and poetry is painting that speaks."

Plutarch

Table of Contents

THUNDER

IN MY

SOUL

a collection of illustrated poems

Introduction

A piece of my heart rests within these pages, it is present in the shared experiences of grief, loss and love. It aches for those in need of comfort and carries a glimmer of hope for those who are bereft. It is yours to keep.

I have always had a love of books. As a child I devoured the stories of Enid Blyton before moving on to Agatha Christie. Like many writers from a previous era they now suffer their share of criticism from those with new values living in a very different world. I however, will always be grateful to them for the hours of enjoyment and escapism they provided in my early years and their introduction to my life long love of a good story.

When poetry was introduced to me in school it demonstrated another way that writers could create stories and provoke emotion in a much more succinct form. It grabbed my attention and fired up my imagination. When we were asked to write our own poems I found the process came naturally, it flowed, it felt familiar, it was enjoyable. I don't remember it being treated as important academically, more a box to be ticked in the curriculum. Once started on this path I continued when others had returned to more familiar ground. My brief scholarly connection with poetry had sparked an interest. It gave me a creative outlet that would remain with me long after I had left formal education. However it wasn't something I ever thought I would share with others, never mind publish.

The poems of my childhood were sparked by the same things they are today, a thought, a random sentence that stays with me, an experience either personal or observed. I can still recall some of my first poems and they have the capability of taking me right back to the moment they were written.

It was the early seventies and I have a clear memory of lying in a field watching the clouds on one of those seemingly never ending days of childhood when a plane passed through my line of vision. Travel wasn't as commonplace as it is now, certainly nothing I'd ever experienced. Apart from an occasional day at the seaside our summers were spent close to home, not that we ever felt we missed out as we weren't any different than most families of the time.

Now when I see a plane, the verse I wrote on that day flows back and I am a child again, it's summer and life is good.

A jet plane flies above my head, its glinting colours blue and red.
I wonder where it's going I say, to some warm country far away.
Carrying people young and old, all over the world so I'm told.
I'd like to fly in one of those, being waited on, curl up my toes.
But oh alas it's home for me, to help my mother make the tea.

The memory still makes me smile.

As I became older, as well as writing poems for myself, I took on the role of the person who wrote the funny, and hopefully insightful, poems for friends birthdays and family celebrations. Not everyone appreciated the humour but I enjoyed it nonetheless. Any poem that was more personal or reflective remained private and if I liked it enough it was kept handwritten in a notebook.

Just as with any activity that is for our own enjoyment, life can often get in the way of its continuance. Marriage, children and work become a priority and we lose the time to pursue our passions and hobbies. There were many years when this was certainly the case for me.

For some, getting that time to create or return to doing the things in life that are just for you can be a gradual process achieved through retirement or children leaving home. Slowly you begin to have space which is yours to fill as you wish.

For others there are pivotal moments which arrive suddenly and unexpectedly and they change our lives in often devastating ways. My pivotal moment was the death of my brother by suicide.

Loss is a personal journey, one that for me has taken many years this far and which I have come to realise will be with me for the rest of my life. At last I have found some peace with that, I am no longer putting life on hold until I am 'over it' for, as anyone who has suffered a profound loss knows, there is no getting over it, but hopefully there is a way to live with it.

The loss of my brother became a catalyst for change in my life. Over the next few years I accepted the fact that I could no longer provide the level of compassion required within my work role. Dealing with other peoples' sadness and distress was preventing me from dealing with my own. I took the decision to leave my job. Now I was adrift and searching for a new direction in my life. It took a while but the day I discovered Sebastian Michaels' *Digital Artistry Course* I knew the next stage of my life was about to begin. I had found my route out of darkness.

No one was more surprised than I was that creating art was the direction my life began to take. I had never seen myself as an artist, I suppose I had a very narrow view of what an artist was and as I couldn't draw or paint I defined myself as non artistic. How crazy was that. Despite my inability to see myself as artistic I could see that others were and that they displayed it in a multitude of ways. There were those who could knit, there were florists, potters, computer game designers, architects, photographers, the list went on and on.

I am thankful that through the discovery of this course I now feel able to call myself a digital artist. Instead of a paintbrush or potters wheel I use a camera and a computer. I have learnt so much over the last few years and yet I have only scratched the surface of what is possible in this medium. As technology grows and develops I know this will be a continuous journey, but as an avid believer in life long learning that suits me just fine.

I began to combine my new digital skills with my poetry and the result is this book of illustrated poems. The poetry I wrote as a child, and still write today, comes not from a deep knowledge of the anatomy of a poem but from the heart. I have not studied the art of poetry in any formal setting but I know what I like to read and what I am moved to write. That is what has influenced the poems contained within this book. I would describe it as a collection of poems based on emotions and life experiences. For those who are curious about the creative process I have included an authors note for each poem along with a quote which I feel reflects the experience or emotion being portrayed.

This is a book born out of grief but it has led to a new contentment. It has been a joy and at times a trauma to create. I hope it is something that people can relate to and be able to get some enjoyment and possibly comfort from.

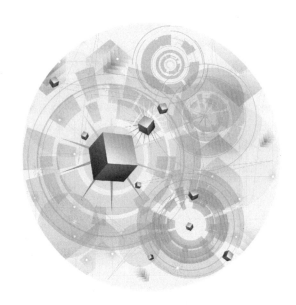

The Thunder in My Soul

"Only passions, great passions can elevate the soul to great things."

Denis Diderot

This poem is about discovering a passion. My discovery was digital art. It has brought such joy to my life and connected me with a group of like minded people all around the world. Alongside that it showed me a way I could illustrate my poetry and led to the creation of this book.

It is wonderful, at any stage in life, to find something that brings so much enjoyment and personal fulfilment. When you find it a little later in life there is an added urgency and desire to learn as much as you can and employ those newly acquired skills in a meaningful way.

For me a passion is something you have to do, you do it for yourself without any agenda. You do it for the pleasure and satisfaction it gives to you. If it leads to an end product you can share with others then that is an added bonus and not the purpose.

Personal experience has taught me that creating can be an uncomfortable process or it can flow. This poem was bit of both, it started with the first line *'there's thunder roaring through me'* replaying over and over in my head. It woke me in the middle of the night, it niggled me during the day until finally the second line came to me and the rest fell into place. The image that accompanies it comes from elements of the poem, the water, the fish and the serenity the creative flow can bring.

The Thunder in My Soul

There's thunder roaring through me
and it's pulling me along.
I feel the rumbling devil drums
I hear the angel song.
A light burns brightly in my heart
I clearly see the way.
The road to my salvation
lies before me on this day.

Slow down, absorb, immerse within,
emerge reborn, cast off old skin.
A thousand sparks, a single fuse
ignites the shy elusive muse.

The wonder of this path I've found
leads me to weep upon the ground.
Then from my tears an ocean grows
and from the ocean fervour flows.
I fall into its depths now free
and all the fishes in the sea
follow where creation leads
so they become the fledgling seeds.

Passion cannot be constrained,
so often beauty's born from pain.
The light's exploding from my soul
and on and on and on it goes.

Take Flight

"To be yourself in a world that is constantly trying to make you something else is the greatest accomplishment."

Ralph Waldo Emerson

Being part of my family has been a largely positive experience, but like many mothers, wives and daughters a lot of my life decisions have been influenced by others needs. Our caring for others can be so ingrained that we feel guilty making a choice that is for us.

There comes a point when it feels like time is running out to do the things that are important to you. You may not even be aware of what it is you want to do, but you know you need the time to find out.

This poem is about that moment when you are brave enough to grasp an opportunity and put your own needs first. You may be surprised to discover that the world doesn't fall apart. Our belief that others expect something different from us or will not be supportive is often misplaced.

Within the image the dispersion of the dandelion seeds in the wind depicts that feeling of freedom experienced from following your own path.

Take Flight

A need for freedom is rising from deep in my core.
The joy in my heart is longing to soar.
With a lifetime of wonder and beauty to share,
this is my chance if only I dare
turn my face to the sun and embrace the light,
take hold of this moment, let go and take flight.
Open my wings and take to the skies,
let go of the guilt and see my passions rise.
Cast off the mask and cry out this is me.
The shackles are broken and I can fly free.

The Mourners Race

'Give sorrow words; the grief that does not speak knits up the over wrought heart and bids it break.'

William Shakespeare

Different cultures grieve in different ways. The first time there is a loss of a loved one within our family we learn from observation how to grieve. We learn what is expected and what is acceptable. We experience the rituals and ceremonies of our communities, which can provide opportunities to talk, to share memories and to vent emotions.

What happens if for some reason we are unable to follow the path we have learnt? We may have moved away from the community we grew up in and left religion and ritual behind. We may have been rendered numb by our loss and feel unable to deal with or process it in any meaningful way for months or even years.

We can be left feeling stranded as others seem to move on and we place expectations on ourselves to do the same. I have certainly felt this pressure after the loss of a loved one. I know a lot of it is self imposed and I know I placed expectations on myself I wouldn't dream of placing on others.

The Mourners Race draws on the feelings generated from being lost in grief. Within the image the skull represents death, the snake represents transition and healing, the hourglass represents how fleeting life is and is also a reference to how there is a time pressure to everything, even grieving.

The Mourners Race

I did not display my grief when it was new,
could not share my true despair with you.
Numbness meant I missed my allotted space,
so here I stand, at the start of the mourners race.

I long to have rituals, permission to roar,
to scream and to rant till the pain is no more.
Can you give me direction a way to begin
to vent all this anguish and let joy back in.

Must my heart stay asleep for a thousand years,
shall my soul stay tied up in chains.
Show me a way to stop this slow death
or dust will be all that remains.

A Miscarriage of Care

"There is a sacredness in tears. They are not the mark of weakness, but of power. They speak more eloquently than ten thousand tongues. They are the messengers of overwhelming grief, of deep contrition, and of unspeakable love."

Washington Irving

As soon as a woman becomes pregnant her child is real to her, a little person with a future and a place in her family. If the pregnancy ends, she has lost a child. At that time of loss and grief it makes no difference to her what stage her pregnancy was at. Every comment made to her will be ingrained in her memory and can affect her ability to move on.

This poem comes from my own experience of such an event and recalls the comments that were made to me at the time by health professionals.

My own miscarriage happened over twenty seven years ago but I can still recall every word that was said to me. It doesn't have the same impact as it did then, time makes changes in your life and we were lucky enough to go on to have a son who has brought us a lot of joy. A son we would not have without our loss.

I would have hoped that health professionals would be more aware now of the impact of poor care at a time of such grief for parents. Having listened to young women who have experienced recent miscarriages, this doesn't always seem to be the case. I would urge those professionals to consider whether they would say to a daughter who has lost her father: *"Well at least you still have your mother"*, to a woman who has lost a sister: *"Be thankful you have another one at home"*, or to a parent whose son died in a car accident: *"Well at least you didn't have to watch him die, that poor woman in the side room has to watch her son die from cancer"*.

It is ridiculous to try and minimise any persons grief by telling them someone else's experience was somehow worse than theirs! Treat them with the respect and sympathy they deserve, and tell them you are sorry they have lost their child. I promise you, it makes a difference.

16

This poem is written from the point of view of a mother, because that is what my experience was. The image depicts the loneliness that is often felt in loss.

A Miscarriage of Care

I lost you
lost my dream of you
of who you would have been.
They said I was lucky.
Lucky I didn't have to deliver you.
Lucky I had a son.
Lucky I could try again.
How could I be lucky.
My baby was dead.

Release

"How people die remains in the memory of those who live on."

Dame Cicely Saunders, founder of the modern hospice movement.

I can never say enough good things about my experience of hospice care. The comfort provided to a terminally ill relative and visiting family members surpassed anything I could have hoped for. It was a place of solace, of compassion and, surprisingly, of hope.

This poem was written while I sat with a relative in such a hospice. It was a very calm and peaceful place and I felt a strong connection to those who had sat there before me. Had they too paced these floors? Had they hoped for a miracle or release for their loved one and themselves? There was a strong sense of the safe haven that would have been provided.

One afternoon, as I sat there quietly, a butterfly appeared. It seemed unusual because it was winter and there was no apparent means by which it could have gained entry to the room. I opened a window and eventually managed to get it to fly out. I am aware that there are many myths and legends surrounding the butterfly and its association with the human spirit. The experience felt really powerful, as if it was a sign that the end was near. I tried to brush the feeling aside, tiredness and sitting in isolation can play tricks on the mind, but almost as predicted the end came early the following morning.

The poem and the image came from my experience of this time. The calmness of the environment, a sense of moving from dark to light, both in going to the hospice where there was relief from pain and worry, and then leaving the physical body for the light of the spiritual world.

Release

I feel the presence of those that have gone before,
hear the restless feet that have paced this floor.
I'm caught in a bubble with emotions that seep
out of the walls of this place as they weep.
They form a cocoon, an embrace from the past.
They whisper, they comfort, the die has been cast.
People now pawns in a game near its end.
We hold our position, we try to defend.
A body so weak it longs for release.
The footsteps are silenced and we have found peace.

Void Ossuary

"Nothing is ever really lost to us as long as we remember it."

L.M. Montgomery, *The Story Girl*.

Having a parent with dementia brings many emotional challenges, you have to adjust your way of thinking, you have to accept that the parent you know is gone and forge a new relationship, accept a new reality. They will never again ask you about your day, enquire after their grandchildren, show an interest in your successes, share in your disappointments.

You have to become a part of the world they now live in, listen to the stories of the places they have been to that day and the people they have seen. Many of the people they talk about will be long departed from your world but live happily in theirs. It can be draining, it can be emotional, especially if you are still grieving for a loved one they see as very much alive. But there is also comfort to be found in this alternative world, for within it your parent can be happy. All their loved ones are with them and all their worries seem to have gone.

This poem refers to some of my experience of this situation.

Within the image the void ossuary, or empty vessel, represents the person who has passed on and the transparent image the person who is still alive but feels invisible.

Void Ossuary

Void ossuary
on ivy bound resting place.
Ash winged keys succumb
to swift release from life's hold,
so death serves the preying flock.

Hope resurrected.
The demons have gone, seeped out
with your memory;
son immortalised by love
while I have ceased to exist.

Shattered Pain

"Mental pain is less dramatic than physical pain, but it is more common and also more hard to bear. The frequent attempt to conceal mental pain increases the burden: it is easier to say 'My tooth is aching' than to say 'My heart is broken.' "

C.S. Lewis

After my brother died everything in the world seemed black. I got no pleasure from the things I had previously enjoyed. The impact was huge. I couldn't read a book, concentrate on a film or enjoy being out in nature. I couldn't talk about it, I couldn't write about it and time has not changed that.

There is a different type of pain associated with losing someone to suicide. The ripples move through families and through years. Although I couldn't write about my personal experience, I recently found a way I could write about this ripple effect on the family left behind.

One evening I accompanied friends to see a Johnny Cash tribute band. Country music can depict life experiences and emotions in quite a detailed way. That night I found the words of a poem forming to the rhythm of the music being played.

The experience enabled me to use the emotion of my loss to tell a story through the voice of a wife who has lost her husband. The result is 'Shattered Pain'. This poem is not autobiographical but it does draw on the reality of losing a family member to suicide. The events are not factual but the devastation is. The image depicts the disintegration and shattering of life.

Shattered Pain

It's ten years since you went away
and we're still picking up the pieces
of the shattered pain that pierced your loved ones' lives.
You thought this world would be better off
without the sadness your life brought
what you didn't realise was it stays behind.

I'm not the woman I used to be
when you left you ripped the heart out of me
all my caring and compassion seemed to go.
A numbness lies inside my chest
there's an empty space where your head should rest
life's simpler when there's nothing left to feel.

Your beautiful boy has become a man.
One anguish ended but another began,
a restless mind can find no peace it seems.
He moves around from place to place
searching for his saving grace
hoping something will give him a reason just to be.

Your little girl is a woman now,
after you left she made a vow
committing to find her own way in this world.
With a promise not to become a wife
anger and sadness consumed her life,
forming a wall to stop love getting in.

Your mothers mind closed down the day
she learnt that you had passed away
unable to cope with the shocking news we brought.
She lives in a past that I don't know
reliving a life from long ago
and the only person that visits her is you.

Your dad hasn't mentioned his only son
from the day the police came and took the gun
that he taught you to use when you were just a child.
He finds some peace in the bottom of a glass
as he sits and waits for time to pass
hoping death will put an end to the guilt he feels.

It's ten years since you went away
and we're still picking up the pieces
of the shattered pain that pierced your loved ones' lives.
You thought this world would be better off
without the sadness your life brought
what you didn't realise was it stays behind.

Hope

"There is no medicine like hope, no incentive so great, and no tonic so powerful as expectation of something tomorrow."

Orison Swett Marden

Even in the depths of grief there are glimmers of light which help you carry on in the hope that better days lie ahead. It can be as simple as the sun breaking through a cloud and just for an instant your heart lifts at the beauty of it. It can be someone letting you know they understand, that they have been there and they have come through. When the whole world seems grey these briefest of moments are everything.

As a witness to someone else's grief you can feel helpless. You may think there is nothing you can do that will make any difference to what they are going through. Nothing you can say that will ease their pain. Contrary to this view I want you to know you could be the person to bring hope, to show a glimpse of the possibility that things can improve. You could be the one that helps someone hold on, that gets them through that hour, that day.

The first year after my brothers death was horrendous, but I expected that. By the second year I thought things would improve and for a while they did. I convinced myself I was progressing normally along a predictable route.

Unfortunately I was to learn grief takes its own path and we are not always in control. Other pressures in your life whether from work or family, can be enough to push you into an abyss you didn't even know you were standing on the edge of. As year three began I plunged into depths from which I thought I would never emerge. Thankfully with time and a glimmer of hope, I did.

There were a number of comments made to me which really helped me put things in perspective and accept that there is no normal way to grieve. No linear path we travel along. Each person is different, each loss is different and you will go through it at whatever pace is right for you. It is not a journey you will ever complete.

One friend shared the fact that it had taken seven years for her to '*get her head round*' losing a sibling in similar circumstances. A work colleague compared grief to a huge black hole that takes over your life leaving room for nothing else, over time it gets smaller and space becomes available for other things, but it never goes away completely. You just live your life around it.

My work roles have always involved an aspect of caring, but now my levels of compassion and empathy became seriously depleted. I felt I was going through the motions but I was not the same person, in work or at home. I shared my frustration at myself with another colleague and her comment was, "W*hen you are drowning you have to save yourself before worrying about anyone else*." This became my mantra when I felt unable to provide the level of support to others that I previously had.

These comments and many other small acts of kindness and compassion are the things that made a difference to me. Never think what you say or do doesn't count, it does.

Hope

Hope walks hand in hand with grief
but makes no mark upon the ground.
Stays a quiet constant presence
waiting calmly to be found.

When my world was at its lowest
and I thought I'd lose my mind,
hope shone from the words of others.
It was patient, wise and kind.

As I surrendered to the night
in that valley of despair,
love spoke to me of mountain tops
and told me hope was there.

I saw the flutter of hopes wings,
a turtle dove in flight.
Reflecting beauty through a haze
of misty mellow morning light.

In that moment I felt comfort
at the centre of my being.
as at last I understood
hope was living in my pain.

Lost

"We remember their love when they can no longer remember."

Unknown

A number of years ago my mother had a stroke, a result of forgetting to take her medication for high blood pressure. Her lack of memory at this time I put down to the effects of grief experienced from the loss of her eldest son. Perhaps it was also partly due to the early stages of dementia, but none of her family were aware of any signs of its presence prior to her stroke. Whatever the cause, we were suddenly plunged into the realities of living with this devastating condition, with all of the emotional turmoil, physical exhaustion, and social constraints it brings.

When you have a loved one who is given the diagnosis of dementia you are very aware of how frightening the early stages of this condition are. You are given a glimpse into what it is like to know your mind and memory are failing, while having the knowledge that it is going to get progressively worse. You become a reluctant witness to the experience of losing the ability to recognise the people you love and losing the skills that allow you to do the things which define who you are. Alongside this you are dealing with your own feelings of what their diagnosis means for you. You are on a journey together over which you have no control.

Everyones experience of dementia is different and the impact on a persons ability to carry out everyday tasks or recall people and places once familiar to them will vary. But no matter what changes occur they are still the person they always were and their feelings remain intact.

This poem and the accompanying image aim to portray the isolation experienced by those who feel they are becoming separated from the world by dementia, while inside they know they are still the person they always were.

Lost

The links to my past are fading,
the path to my future unclear.
I'm stranded; alone and frightened.
I'm screaming but no one can hear.

In the mirror I see an old woman,
she's someone that I used to know.
A girl holds my hand and keeps smiling
and I cry when she gets up to go.

I've no memories but I'm still a person.
I've no words but I've something to say.
I've no family but I'm still a mother.
I've no God but I still need to pray.

Crafting with Mother

"Memory … is the diary that we all carry about with us."

Oscar Wilde

I spent a morning sitting with my mother making a hedgehog out of an old book. Not something I had ever imagined I would do.

It was in a nursing home and my mother had dementia. We were taking part in one of the many activities provided for residents as a way of stimulating the brain and providing some exercise for hands and fingers.

This is an excellent home and my reflections are in no way a criticism of it or the activities provided. However, no matter how excellent care is, there are always moments as a relative when the reality of a situation is brought home to you and this was one of them for me.

As we made our hedgehogs, every few minutes one of the participants would ask the question, *"What is this for?"*. The activities co-ordinator would reply, *"It will provide a place to keep reminders of appointments, letters and family photographs"*.

Although the hedgehogs were to be sold and would be used by those that purchased them, the poignancy of that repeated question and reply, was quite profound. This poem is a result of that experience.

The image represents being lost and adrift with no memory of who you are or were. Included are images of the hedgehogs made from the old books. Falling from the pages and lost in the depths of the ocean are the reminders and family photographs that no longer hold any meaning.

Crafting with Mother

By folding back the pages of a book
we crafted a hedgehog mother and I.
Endless repetition, what use has this.

Place photographs of family you miss.
Reminders to prevent plans going awry,
in between the spines of the hedgehog book.

There is no memo that will clear the mist,
No aide memoir on which we can rely.
No hope. Repeat again what use has this.

Objects can be a way to reminisce.
But dull synapses won't be sharpened by
the conscious pricking of the hedgehog book.

When memories fall into an abyss
there are no craft can venture where they lie.
If they are lost from us, what use has this.

You look at me and you are there. Remiss
I start to ask the foolish question, why
am I not in the pages of the book,
and if I can't be there what use has this.

Tales of My Father

Gilbert K. Chesterton

When we were children, my father was a great storyteller, it was hard to tell fact from fiction in some of his more dramatic tales. Perhaps it ran in the family, for when his brother came to visit he would terrify us with his stories of ghosts and vampires.

We lived in an old house and when my uncle was there we would sit around the open fire, the only other light flickering from a gas lamp. The house was surrounded by trees, and when he spoke in a hushed voice the wind always seemed to be howling as the rain beat against the windows, adding an extra layer of fear. We would all be so quiet, straining to hear every word, the drama would build and build eventually coming to a sudden end with a scream, a loud noise or my uncle pointing to a supposed face he could see at the window. We would almost jump out of our skin with fear, but we couldn't get enough of his scary stories.

Deep down we knew it was all fiction, but with my father we were never quite sure. There was always an element of plausibility, but every time he told a story a little bit more would be added. There was one about the really bad winter where the snow came to the top of the church wall. In the next version it came up to the roof until eventually the only thing that could be seen was the top of the church spire peaking through the snow.

Then there was the local eccentric who drove his tractor into a flood so deep it was almost completely immersed. He could not be persuaded to leave the vehicle and instead stood on the small part still visible above the raging water, saluted and proclaimed, "A captain always goes down with his ship". Every tale was embellished, a little exaggeration always made for a better story.

This poem is my own, perhaps embellished, memories of the tales he told. I think perhaps we all inherited a little of his storytelling ways, some perhaps more than others. I will leave it up to my siblings to decide for themselves who became the biggest embellisher of us all and I don't think it was me. As was often said it doesn't do to let the truth get in the way of a good story.

The image is made to represent a tapestry which includes references to the stories from the poem.

Tales of My Father

My father's a spinner of colourful
yarns. His creations can seem quite absurd.
But just sit a while in his company
and you'll enter a magical world.

I've seen dragons fly high in formation
to roar fire at the evil knight.
When they save the princess from certain death
I join in their triumphant flight.

I've walked on the moon, played catch with the stars
and travelled through light years in space.
I've spent all day hanging out with the clouds
and come first in a floating race.

I've swam with the fish, heard animals talk,
performed in a circus with clowns.
I'm so entwined in the pattern he weaves
I'm part of the tapestry now.

The History of Tea (and Me) - I

"If man has no tea in him, he is incapable of understanding truth and beauty."

Japanese Proverb

The starting point for the following two poems came from my giving some thought to the connections I have had with tea throughout my life.

This led to my looking further back into the history of tea in general, where it originated and how it came to be so linked with the very idea of Britishness.

I did a little research into the subject and the following poem is the condensed version of what I discovered. The image is a pictorial record of the journey tea made from its origins to the heart of London.

The History of Tea (and Me) - I

What a happy accident beneath the Camellia tree.
Leaves blew off, water boiled, suddenly it's tea.
Buddhist monks, Japanese, on a study tour
liked the brew, took it home, rituals endure.

The Europeans, slow at first, then word travelled through,
the Dutch brought tea from China, from there the fashion grew.
When Charles the Second married his Portuguese princess,
she brought with her a taste for tea, with which she was obsessed.

Within the Court and upper class a love of tea began.
High cost lowered consumption in the common working man.
The consequence was smuggling and criminality.
Pitt the Younger slashed the tax, everyone had tea.

Time moved on, those idle rich found reason to rejoice,
tea instead of alcohol could be the workers choice.
During war, the government, aimed to boost morale,
ensured tea was imported, a perfect rationale.

Many bonds created in harmony and strife
as tea became established in the British way of life.

shrub, *Camellia sinensis*, of eastern Asia

te, equivalent of Mandarin *cha*

tea An aromatic, slightly bitter drink made by steeping tea leaves in boiling water.

The History of Tea (and Me) - II

"If you are cold, tea will warm you; if you are too heated, it will cool you; If you are depressed, it will cheer you; if you are excited, it will calm you."

William E. Gladstone

Tea is the thread that runs throughout my life, providing a connection to each part. Something I don't see changing anytime soon, at least I do hope not. It has been present at all those major and minor events that have been part of my journey to date.

The times I spent with my granny as she taught me her sewing skills, something which I unfortunately seem to have lost along the way.

Those nightmare years of potato gathering. Being a farmers daughter meant there was no choice involved. The only relief from this imposed labour was when my mother arrived with sustenance at lunchtime and mid-afternoon. She really did go above and beyond the call of duty. There were many grateful recipients of the hot Irish stew and afternoon sandwiches. For me it was the mug of hot tea that provided a very welcome respite.

What mother who has just given birth doesn't remember that first cup of tea? No other one will ever taste as good.

So many occasions would be incomplete without it, so many memories of good times and bad are formed over a cuppa.

This poem is my recollection of the role tea has played in my life. The image includes the sofa I sat on at my granny's and the sewing box she used. The decorative work in the linen is hers along with all the other pieces displayed. With my tea there was always buttered brown bread and homemade jam, usually marmalade. Those were happy days.

The History of Tea (and Me) - II

Visiting granny, the heat of the fire, learning to crochet and bake.
The only sound the tick of the clock and the crackle the logs would make.
Home made jam, buttered brown bread, tea from a china pot.
Crisp white linen, silver that shone, scones that were served while hot.

Drill filled fields that met the sky, my own potato blight.
Days that seemed to stretch for ever, the fleeting calm of night.
On the horizon a glimmer of hope came walking at twelve and three,
lie down in the soil, stretch out with the worms, salvation is served with tea.

Visiting wakes, the shaking of hands, a way to remember the dead.
Dressed in their best the departed host lies at peace on the bed.
The rattle of cups, the pouring of tea, sandwiches served from a tray.
Stories are shared but laughter subsides when the minister starts to pray.

Childhood memories, leaving home, first love that came to an end.
A hard day at work, a baby's first cry, sharing bad news with a friend.
Finding my passion, living my dream, getting back up when I fall.
Tea – the constant thread in my life, the beginning and end of it all.

One Kiss

"How did it happen that their lips came together? How does it happen that birds sing, that snow melts, that the rose unfolds, that the dawn whitens behind the stark shapes of trees on the quivering summit of the hill? A kiss, and all was said."

Victor Hugo

Fate brought my now husband and I together in the early eighties in Belfast. He had travelled from England to work for a few weeks. In those days Northern Ireland was not a place most people would choose to visit. He was young, just out of university, and the only one from his workplace prepared to venture over.

My brother worked for the same company so it was inevitable our paths would cross at some point. We had met a few times but never dated, yet a spontaneous kiss as he left a party was all it took for me to know my future was sealed. Within six months we were engaged and nine months later we married.

A few of the poems within this collection have been created in the Japanese poetic form of a tanka. A tanka consists of five lines, each with a mandatory number of syllables. It translates as 'short song' and is an ancient form of Japanese poetry which began in the seventh century. It was often used for emotional expression.

I enjoy the challenge of communicating a feeling or experience using this brief form of verse and felt it would work in the context of this poem. A few words can convey all you need to say.

The poem is about the moment you know you have found the person you hope to spend the rest of your life with and how that initial bond deepens over time.

The image depicts the kiss that could be the start of everything we wish for in life. Peace, contentment, knowing you are with the right person and stronger because of it.

One Kiss

One kiss let me know
you were not a passing phase.
Now a look's enough
to let you see my passion
has not diminished with time.

A Peaceful Sanctuary

"Peace comes from within. Do not seek it without".

Gautama Buddha

One thing I hope my children will achieve in life is contentment, that feeling of being at peace with who and where you are.

Contentment is not something that can be guaranteed through academic or financial success. There are many wealthy, seemingly successful people, who are still looking for that elusive something to prove to themselves and others that they have made it. They believe that when they find this unknown entity or achieve this unnamed goal then they will be truly happy.

Happiness and contentment are different things and we should acknowledge that it is impossible to be happy all of the time, but it is possible to be content with what we have and who we are. Instead of looking for things to add to our lives we should be looking at what we already have and be thankful. Instead of focusing on our perceived failures we should be celebrating our successes.

We are fortunate in so many aspects of our lives: where we live, the friends we have and the many acts of kindness we witness. We need to notice these and be grateful for them.

This is a poem about how we often look to others to provide us with that feeling of peace and contentment.

If we are unhappy we blame our work, our relationships, our finances – basically anything other than looking within ourselves to find the answers and discover what we could do differently to effect the change we crave. The only person who can bring about change in our lives is us.

A Peaceful Sanctuary

A peaceful sanctuary
to calm my restless mind.
I thought that you would be
a peaceful sanctuary.
Instead love set me free,
to look inside and find
a peaceful sanctuary
to calm my restless mind

Powerless Without Love

"It is worth remembering that the time of greatest gain in terms of wisdom and inner strength is often that of greatest difficulty."

Dalai Lama

There has been a lot of content in the media in recent years about mental health and the need for better support and treatment. You may assume therefore that services have improved and there is a better understanding within the general public. Unfortunately we are not at that stage yet.

There is still a perceived stigma and a general lack of knowledge about what mental health entails. This ignorance makes it difficult for family and friends to provide any meaningful support. It also makes it almost impossible for those who are suffering to share their experience, for fear of being judged unfairly.

Those who have cared for, lived with, or have a friend who has endured any form of mental ill health, will understand the struggle of wanting to help but not always being able to. Many will recognise the feeling of thinking you are powerless. It is important not to lose sight of the fact that just being available to listen and not judge can make a difference. You don't have to have all the answers. Often it is only love that can carry us through.

Powerless Without Love

In the face of your despair,
    I am powerless.

In the face of your delusion,
    I am powerless.

In the face of your rage,
    I am powerless.

In the face of your desire to leave this world,
    I am powerless.

In the face of your belief that you are unloveable,
    I am powerful beyond words.

Love gives me strength.

Love gives me patience.

Love gives me hope.

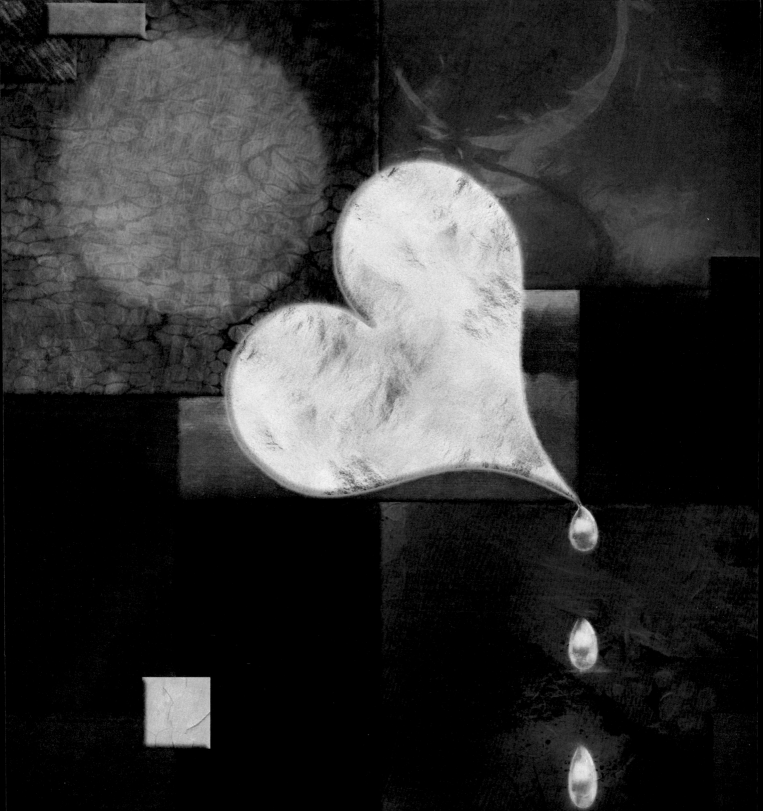

Spring

"The butterfly counts not months but moments, and has time enough."

Rabindranath Tagore

Spring is a time of new beginnings, of hope for the future. For me spring arrives with the cherry blossom. I love its delicate nature, soft colours and wonderful scent. Part of its beauty is in its fragility, it is so vulnerable to the moods of the weather.

The poem is a play on the idea of the fragility of the flower and the fragility of love and life itself. Things that mean so much to us can be gone in an instant. The essence, those qualities that form the core of a person or a blossom may dissipate, but the memory will linger to bring comfort in the dark days that follow.

In Japan the cherry blossom is held in high esteem and is seen to reflect the Buddhist themes of mortality, mindfulness and living in the present. The flower is a symbol of Japan's most deep-rooted cultural and philosophical beliefs.

It is unlikely I will get to travel to Japan anytime soon to witness for myself the wondrous vision of hundreds of cherry blossoms blooming en masse. So for now I am content to enjoy the sight of a single tree with its pink flowers juxtaposed against a clear blue sky on a bright spring day, however fleeting that may be.

Spring

Fragile pink blossom.
The north wind left me bereft.
Your presence too brief.
Sweet essence, a memory
that brings solace in the night.

Summer

"You must live in the present, launch yourself on every wave, find your eternity in each moment. Fools stand on their island of opportunities and look toward another land."

Henry David Thoreau

Summer can be seen as a representation of our youth, where time seems to stretch before us endlessly and opportunities are present in abundance. They are often viewed as heady days where we are full of energy with a thirst for adventure and a willingness to grab every chance to live life to the full.

That is certainly true for some people but not everyone. Some will be more cautious in their approach to life. That can be wise at times but if it leads to regrets then we can look back in later years and be frustrated with our former selves.

We are convinced that if only we could combine the wisdom we have gained with age with the vitality of our youth we would have the perfect combination. This thought process can only lead to more wasted years.

We should use our time wisely and take the opportunities available to us. Otherwise, we may find ourselves looking back with the same regrets at the next stage of our lives.

The image is a vision of a perfect summer day spent with loved ones, without a care in the world. Savour those moments when they come. This is a compilation of images taken in St Ives, Cornwall, a wonderful atmospheric place which I would urge you to visit if given the opportunity.

Summer

Life stretched before us
in those long hot days of youth.
You danced in the light.
I looked for darkening skies
fearing storms that never came.

Autumn

"Why is it that so many of us persist in thinking that autumn is a sad season? Nature has merely fallen asleep, and her dreams must be beautiful if we are to judge by her countenance."

Samuel Taylor Coleridge

Autumn is a time of fading beauty, where opportunity and golden moments still exist if we take the time to look. It can represent a time of diminishing life, so as the crops become depleted and gathered in so it may seem do the lives of those around us and our belief in the possibility of a new chapter for ourselves.

Contrary to this somewhat negative view these years can be about gratitude and fulfilment. If we are lucky enough to still have a healthy body and mind then we should celebrate it. Instead of regretting the time that is gone we need to be thankful that we have made it this far.

No one knows when the end of their journey will come, there are no guarantees, but you can choose to live the best life you can right now. This is your time to reap your own harvest, to develop new skills or rediscover old passions and start anew.

The image depicts the fading beauty of an Autumn evening. The last fruits glisten, waiting for those who still have the energy, to grasp them.

Autumn

The last golden fruit
glistens in the setting sun.
Shorter days beckon.
Your eyes dim as the light fades,
I am alone in the dark.

Winter

"I wonder if the snow loves the trees and fields, that it kisses them so gently? And then it covers them up snug, you know, with a white quilt; and perhaps it says, 'Go to sleep, darlings, till the summer comes again'."

Lewis Carroll, *Alice's Adventures in Wonderland*

Winter can be a time of cold and desolation, creating a bare land with a bleak outlook. It has been compared to the final stages of our lives or to periods of emotional distress where everything seems grey and hopeless.

At these times we need to remember that like all of the seasons it too will pass. We will discover that beneath the surface of the snow and ice or the despair we feel, there are seeds of life and hope waiting for the opportunity to bloom and grow again.

The image depicts the coldness of winter but also that there is still beauty to be found and life to be lived. In the darkest of days there is light.

Winter

A flurry of snow.
Children laughing as they play,
immune to the cold.
Beneath the blanket of stars
tender buds of love take root.

Thoughts of Home

"Where we love is home – home that our feet may leave, but not our hearts."

Oliver Wendell Holmes Sr.

What makes a home? Is it a place, or a state of mind?

For some people it's a country for some it's a specific house, for others it is a person or people, or a feeling of contentment.

For most it is probably a combination of these things. I'm sure it can be fluid and change over time. It is inevitable we will be influenced by our personal life experiences.

Living and working in different environments, moving away from our birth family, new loves and new countries – these things will all influence what home means to us. Yet at the core will remain whatever it is that gives you that elusive feeling of knowing you are where you are meant to be.

This poem captures what home is for me. Everyone will have their own image of their ideal home in their head. What is yours?

Thoughts of Home

When I think of home there's always you
and flowers that gleam in the morning dew.
A roaring fire, a glass of wine,
side by side your hand in mine.

A dog at our feet, a book to be read.
Knowing I'm loved without it being said.
The sound of rain in the dead of night,
the comforting glow from a bedside light.

Home is a feeling, a sense I belong,
where I can be me, and I can be wrong.
A place I am known, where I don't just exist.
A place I am welcome, a place I am missed.

It's memories and moments that live in my soul.
It's peace and contentment, it's where I am whole.

Wish You Were Here

"Take the first step in faith. You don't have to see the whole staircase, just take the first step."

Dr. Martin Luther King Jr.

Are there things in your life you wish you had done differently? Decisions you made you would like to change? Or do you take a more pragmatic approach seeing everything as a learning experience.

Do you look back at your younger self with understanding and compassion, recognising that you made the best decision you could at the time with the knowledge and life experience you had, or do you continually berate yourself for what you see as past mistakes?

Perhaps it is a mixture of both and perhaps it depends on whether your decision adversely affected others.

These things interest me, what makes some people analyse every word they said in every situation, while others never give the past a second thought? We are all wired differently but I think we can train our thought process to fall somewhere in the middle of these extremes.

To achieve anything worthwhile we have to allow ourselves to take risks, if things don't turn out as we hoped we need to be able to accept that as part of life, learn what we can from the experience, and move on.

I don't have any major regrets in my life but like most people there have been occasions when fear of what might happen has informed my decision. I am lucky in that I enjoy change and new challenges and I have become braver with age and experience.

It is said more people regret the things they didn't do in life than the things they did. So be honest with yourself, are you doing what you want to do or is fear preventing you? Do you want to live with regret or take a chance and be able to say at least I tried? Stop waiting for the right moment to say what you want to say, or do what you want to do, for the right moment is now.

After the first line of this poem came to me I spent some time thinking about whose voice it represented. An image of an elderly man kept appearing in my mind and the voice became his. The unexpected sight of a young woman crying causes him to reflect back on his life, his regrets and the gift of finding love. The image is a representation of the imagined scene that set his thoughts in motion.

Wish You Were Here

I saw a girl with tears in her eyes
and it made me think of you.
Of how careless I sometimes treated our love
when it was still brand new.

I longed to say to the man at her side
take her hand, dry her tears,
hold her tight. You won't always have tomorrow,
day can turn into endless night.

I was a fool but you stayed through the years
and made me the best I could be.
Thank God you saw what I could become and your
love took a chance on me.

My beautiful girl; I wish you were here.
This old heart holds such an ache.
I trust you are waiting somewhere for me and I
long for our new dawn to break.

Mother Dear

"Children need models rather than critics."

Joseph Joubert

Parenting is hard, so unsurprisingly we don't always get it right. Long days and sleepless nights can cause us to manage children's behaviour in ways that probably wouldn't be found in the pages of a parenting manual.

Having taught parenting classes and worked with parents for many years I know the majority want to do a good job. I also know that even the best of them don't always live up to their own aspirations.

Our children don't always behave as we would wish and neither do we! None of us are perfect and that's OK. Forgive yourself, be kind to yourself and do the same for your children. You may not be perfect but you'll be good enough.

This is a light-hearted look at how parents can often have expectations of their children that they don't seem to have for themselves. The mother portrayed has a bit of a 'do as I say not as I do' attitude.

While my own mother had very high standards regarding her children's behaviour, she also had those expectations for herself and would certainly not have behaved as the mother depicted within this poem. So I can't say this is written from any personal experience I may have had as a child and I hope my own children wouldn't say it's how I have been as a parent, at least not all of the time.

Mother Dear

Oh mother dear you taught me well
and I am now a perfect girl,
who's always kind and so polite,
who never cheats and never fights,
who knows to never tell a lie
and that's the honest reason why.

I told Aunt Jo you think she's fat.
Gosh she got quite upset at that.
She said you told her she looked great
carrying some extra weight.

Dad's gone out to clear his head.
I accidentally moved your bed,
which suddenly exposed the sight
of what you buy online at night.

Gran doesn't mind you take her car.
I said we never drive too far,
but still she seemed surprised to hear
you changed the mileage clock last year.

I think your boss might be upset.
He asked if you were better yet.
I said that you were feeling great
in Malaga with your best mate.

Don't worry, as you've said to me,
just take responsibility.
Apologise, say you were wrong,
and hopefully, before too long
they'll see forgiveness is divine.
For no one's perfect all the time.

Except me …

A Dress of Roses

I love to photograph flowers and I am always trying to find new ways I can create art from the process.

To form my dress of roses I placed the rose petals on a light box to illuminate them from behind, giving them an ethereal look. I digitally combined the resulting photographs with other images to create a beautiful dress suspended from a branch.

I loved the resulting artwork and found myself imagining what it would be like to wear such a dress on your wedding day. The accompanying poem is the result of these deliberations.

A Dress of Roses

On our wedding day I wore a dress of roses,
the velvet petals soft against my skin.
Their heady scent engulfed us at the altar
as we waited for our new life to begin.

A rainbow bridge cascaded through the window.
It formed a path to where the angels sing.
United their voices joined the chorus
in celebration of what pure love can bring.

A shimmering luminance was emanating
from the gown of blossoms forming my bouquet.
Some fell upon the aisle as we were leaving.
Fading memories from a perfect day.

Look at Me

I liked the rose dress so much that I went on to create a series of flower dresses. Not all of them have as yet inspired poems but this one created from daisies and buttercups did.

The process began in a similar way, the flowers were photographed separately on a light box before being combined digitally. However it was a much more complex process, with each flower being individually placed into position to form the finished dress.

Daisies and buttercups grow in abundance throughout our grass and are often seen as weeds to be eradicated, but I love the colour and vibrancy of them. After I had completed the image I began to think of how often flowers and plants that are categorised as weeds can be quite beautiful if we just take the time to really look at them.

It is often only because someone else has designated plants and flowers as weeds that we look at them in such a negative way. This poem is a commentary on that but also on how we can view people and entire cultures in a negative way because of our own upbringing and life experience. It is important for us to see the world through our own eyes, not someone else's.

Look at Me

I bring a beauty to the world you can't rejoice in.
I exist beyond your narrow point of view.
You dismiss me as something unimportant.
I deserve more than a fleeting glance from you.

I am a glorious cacophony of colour.
The vibrant light of nature shines from me.
There is splendour in every little detail.
Take the time to look and you will see.

Release your senses from the limits of your culture.
An overwhelming wonder lies outside.
The constraints you've placed upon your vision
will crumble like castles in the tide.

I Will Paint the Sky for You

"Love is a canvas furnished by nature and embroidered by imagination."

Voltaire

This is a poem about love.

The word love is used in so many different situations, with different connotations attached. It can become almost meaningless through overuse. We talk of loving many things. We 'love' our friends, our children, the latest movie, a good book and if we are lucky our job. Each one of these 'loves' will have a different feeling attached to it.

It probably doesn't matter how often and in what context we use the word love as long as we have the emotional literacy to define the varying feelings attached to each person or experience.

By being mindful of our feelings, when a great romantic love arrives unexpectedly into our life, we are more likely to recognise it for what it is. We will see what lies beyond the passion, we will do what we can to nurture and develop what we have been given. We will see the need to value and protect it. We will be willing to make sacrifices and compromises. We will commit to longevity. Every day we will know we love and are loved by how we behave and how we are treated. That is the love this poem is about.

The image and poem portray the desire of the human heart to discover concrete means by which they are able to portray the depth of their feelings to another.

I Will Paint the Sky for You

I am a painter.
I will paint the sky for you
with tender strokes of love
in yellow, gold and blue.

I am a gardener.
I will plant a field of flowers
and lie with you at midnight
in a bed beneath the stars.

I am a builder.
I will forge a fort from stone
and place it on a mountain top
so you will have a home.

I am a singer.
I will sing a song so sweet
that birds will pause in wonder
and sirens crumble in defeat.

I am a dancer.
I will sway beneath the sun
and move with you in harmony
until we fuse as one.

I am a poet
with a passion to ignite
your soul with words of tenderness
that set your heart alight.

Songbird Silenced

"What lies behind us and what lies before us are tiny matters compared to what lies within us."

Ralph Waldo Emerson

In 1981 a social worker defined a new term 'the sandwich generation'. It referred to adults, mainly in their thirties and forties, who were raising young children and supporting ageing parents.

Over the years, partly due to women postponing having children and the elderly living longer, the sandwich generation now includes adults in their fifties and sixties.

These are people who are financially and practically supporting adult children while also caring for elderly parents.

Combine those demands with a job and running a home and the pressure can become unbearable. There can be a lot of guilt. You can feel pulled in many directions and even though you are doing the best you can, it often feels like you don't have the time to do all that needs to be done. Who cares for the carers? Quite often the answer is no one.

We can all feel weighed down by expectations and responsibilities. I have certainly felt overwhelmed at times and this poem is about those feelings. The image represents the idea of escaping from a cage formed by others needs.

Songbird Silenced

Reach inside my head old friend
there's something I can't find.
Others needs, demands and wants
have cluttered up my mind.

Seek out the captive bird in
there: feathers dull and grey,
singing silenced through bars formed
by men with feet of clay.

When you locate this weary
soul, trust you have the key.
Open up that gilded cage
and set the songbird free.

Snapshots

"Memory is the treasury and guardian of all things."

Marcus Tullius Cicero

Photoshop is one of a number of digital programmes I use to create my art. One of the functions it has is the ability for the artist to take a snapshot of enhancements they have made to an image at any point in their workflow. This provides a temporary copy. They can then continue working and take further snapshots of progress as they wish. Finally they can compare each version before deciding which one to keep.

Imagine if we could do this in our lives. What if you were at a point in your life where you were content but you had an opportunity to take a different direction. Would you be more likely to try something new if you could take a snapshot which you could return to if you weren't happy with the outcome of your decision?

That could be quite tempting, but unfortunately it's not going to happen. What we can do though is take time to focus on when we are happy and store those moments as memories or 'snapshots' which we can draw on when life gets a little bit tougher.

This poem and accompanying image developed from that idea. It's about the importance of reflecting on our positive memories. We often have the habit of looking at negative experiences or worrying about what we may have done differently. The mind is a powerful thing and we need to use it wisely and to our benefit.

Snapshots

I keep snapshots in my memory
tucked carefully out of sight,
of special moments from my past
when everything felt right.

I've got the night I met you there,
the moment when I knew,
that all the plans I'd made before
now held a place for you.

Our wedding day, the love we felt,
the roses and the lace.
My certainty that all of life
had led me to this place.

The birth of both our children.
How love expands and grows.
Our hope they'd find contentment
on whatever path they chose.

I store the things I'm grateful for
so when the dark days come,
I play the snapshots in my mind,
relive them one by one.

No life holds only happiness.
All love will bring some pain.
But the memory of the sunshine
can't be washed away by rain.

The Wondering Hour

I've always been a light sleeper and an early riser. The early rising is a legacy of being a farmer's daughter. As a child if you lay in bed beyond eight in the morning, you were woken none too gently to be informed half the day was gone and you were in peril of wasting the rest of it.

As I have become older I have developed an unfortunate tendency to waken in the early hours of the morning, unable to get back to sleep I begin to replay past events in my mind. I spend time wondering if there was anything I should have or could have done differently. You could argue this is a redundant pastime but I prefer to think I am learning from my perceived mistakes and this will improve how I react in a similar situation in the future. You can convince yourself of anything at three in the morning.

Combine the light sleeping and the replaying of events with being of a certain age and a lot of sleepless nights are inevitable. This poem is a result of a few such nights, so even those hours are not wasted. My father would be pleased about that. Within the image I wanted to portray the idea of a nightmare while also referencing elements from the poem.

The Wondering Hour

Awake again in the wondering hour,
that sleepy, creepy slumbering hour,
where goblins crawl around my bed
and past ghosts sneak inside my head.

They twist and turn and won't be still,
determined to overcome my will
and free the fear within my core
then feed it and knead it and open the door
so it can reach every part of my being,
capture my mind and give it free reign.

Fear conjures spirits from the shimmering gloom,
two realms converge within this one room.
Where are you now you reluctant sheep
I've constructed the fences, you just have to leap.
I count on you all but you never come,
so I lie and I wait for the rising sun.

Deliverance arrives with the morning light
to signal the end of another night.
The goblins retreat, the ghosts fade away,
the spirits return to their world for the day.
I'm left alone in awe of the power
of the dark and the mind and the wondering hour.

The Ghosts of Our Memories

"Memories warm you up from the inside. But they also tear you apart."

Haruki Murakami, *Kafka on the Shore*

Have you ever walked around an old house and been curious about its past? Once it would have been filled with laughter, tears and all of the emotion that families bring. It always feels so sad to see a house that has been abandoned and allowed to become derelict when at some time it must have meant so much to someone.

When I visit old houses, whatever their current state, I can't help thinking about whether these buildings that have seen so many lives pass through them hold onto the memories of their former occupants. Could the moods of the families who have lived there be absorbed into the walls? Do such houses make us feel happy or sad depending on the experiences of its previous inhabitants?

This poem is inspired by my own family home but it encompasses all such buildings. It reflects the idea that a house lives the life of those who reside within its walls. That it is affected by the emotions, life stages and health of its inhabitants. As they deteriorate and age, so does it. The house begins to long for the youth and vibrancy of a new family to bring it back to life and its former glory.

It's also about how we feel the memories of our childhood intensified when we visit the home we grew up in. How we often absorb the sadness we imagine the house feels due to the changes the passing of time has brought. It's as if the ghosts of our childhood, the memories and the lives we once lived, are all around us as we walk through the rooms.

The Ghosts of Our Memories

The house holds its breath as I walk through the silent rooms.
Longing for revival it slumps beneath the weight of too
many years of sadness, resentment building year by year.
Time passing, youth fading, hoping for a new start, a new heart.

Here where the sun falls gently through the window, I sat with Enid and Agatha
nurturing the growth of a passion for adventure and new worlds.
Riding our steeds around King Arthur's table, our own little band of five fought
as Jim Reeves played, but always we stayed united against the world.

A place of magic, where once a year we crept down creaking stairs, oil lamps
lighting the way, visible breath dissipated by the open fire. A time of wonder.
Here was freedom, trees to climb, dens to build, a childhood set to the
soundtrack of laughter as the beat of a ball repeated against the garden wall.

Trepidation lurked in the attic with forgotten furniture beneath ghost like shrouds.
Through dense cobwebs eyes stared from portraits of those long forgotten
as they forged a new existence in nightmares and fertile imaginations.
Bats slumbered in the shadows knowing their feast would come with the setting sun.

Here, the door I walked through on my wedding day, the garden where we stood
beneath the cherry blossom. Here we gathered to celebrate the milestones that
came with the passing of time, to remember how it was and wonder where it went.
Here we arrived with the dawn to break the news the first born was gone.

Here we sat in shocked silence and never spoke of pain. Here a mother
lost her mind as love and duty merged and the cared for became the carers.
Here life became a waiting game for a peace that could never come.
Here the ghosts of memories lie but none give the answer to the question.

Why?

Acknowledgements

Thank you to all of the artists for the wonderful resources provided through Sebastian Michaels' Photoshop Artistry courses.

Sebastian Michaels, your excellent training, content, and ongoing encouragement provided through your courses gave me the skills which allowed me to bring this project to completion, I will always be grateful.

To my *Awake Group* of fellow artists, thank you for your constant encouragement and support. You have reinforced my belief that the human race is inherently good and shown me that you don't have to meet a person to know they are a kindred spirit.

To Becky, thank you for fine tuning my final draft. Your editorial input and encouraging comments were so helpful.

Special thanks to my husband Keith, for his constant encouragement throughout the development of this book, for his editorial and formatting input, for pushing me to keep going, for believing I could do it when I didn't think I could and for taking me dancing and making me laugh.

Art Credits

In creating the illustrative art pieces within this book the author used her own images and a variety of elements from other sources as detailed below.

ClipArtLord.com public domain images page 47.

PixelSquid elements are included on pages 7, 8, 12, 15,19, 20, 24, 27, 40, 47, 48, 52, 56, 60,64,68,72,76, 80, 84, 96, 99,100, 103, 104, 107, 108, 115, 116, 119.

Rebecca McMeen elements pages 36 and 112.

Sebastian Michaels model images pages 79 and 91.

Teddi Rutschman elements are included on pages 9, 13, 23, 43, 51, 55, 111, 119 and 120.

Various elements and textures are from artists who provide content for students within Sebastian Michaels' Photoshop Artistry courses.

About the Author

Inspired by personal and observed experiences of life, love and loss Norma Slack weaves a unique and moving combination of art and the written word. Each individual pairing of image and poem has the power to evoke emotion and empathy. They speak of topics we can all relate to. Norma has worked in numerous roles, including nursing and parent support, but most of the influence for this book has come from her personal life.

Norma was born and grew up in Northern Ireland where she completed her nursing and midwifery training. In the early years of work and marriage she moved to England to live. The call of home remained strong and in 1990 she returned with her family to her birth place. She currently lives in County Down, within view of the majestic Mourne mountains and has been married to Keith for over thirty years. They have two sons.

Norma has had images published in the magazine '*Living The Photo Artistic Life*' and is a member of Sebastian Michaels Awake group of digital artists. Her art can be viewed online at '*www.normasue.com*'. Thunder in My Soul is her first book.

Made in the USA
Lexington, KY
14 May 2018